JUL - 1 2016

3 1994 01551 4612

SANTA ANA PUBLIC LIBRARY

D0633809

THE
COLONIAL
PERIOD

THE COLONIAL PERIOD

J 973.3 COL
The colonial period

$32.90
CENTRAL   31994015514612

EDITED BY
JAMES WOLFE

Britannica
Educational Publishing

IN ASSOCIATION WITH

ROSEN
EDUCATIONAL SERVICES

Published in 2016 by Britannica Educational Publishing (a trademark of Encyclopædia Britannica, Inc.) in association with The Rosen Publishing Group, Inc.
29 East 21st Street, New York, NY 10010

Copyright © 2016 by Encyclopædia Britannica, Inc. Britannica, Encyclopædia Britannica, and the Thistle logo are registered trademarks of Encyclopædia Britannica, Inc. All rights reserved.

Rosen Publishing materials copyright © 2016 The Rosen Publishing Group, Inc. All rights reserved.

Distributed exclusively by Rosen Publishing.

To see additional Britannica Educational Publishing titles, go to rosenpublishing.com.

First Edition

Britannica Educational Publishing
J.E. Luebering: Director, Core Reference Group
Anthony L. Green: Editor, Compton's by Britannica

Rosen Publishing
Christine Poolos: Editor
Nelson Sá: Art Director
Michael Moy: Designer
Cindy Reiman: Photography Manager
Karen Huang: Photo Researcher

Library of Congress Cataloging-in-Publication Data

The colonial period / edited by James Wolfe.
    pages cm. -- (Early American history)
 Audience: Grades 7-12.
 Includes bibliographical references and index.
 ISBN 978-1-68048-268-3 (library bound)
 1. United States—History—Colonial period, ca. 1600-1775—Juvenile literature. I. Wolfe, James, 1960-
 E188.C724 2016
 973.3—dc23

                                                                        2015016992

Manufactured in the United States of America

Photo Credits: Cover, p. 3 Photo 12/Universal Images Group/Getty Images; pp. 7, 14-15, 33 Encyclopaedia Britannica, Inc.; pp. 11, 41, 44-45, 50 MPI/Archive Photos/Getty Images; pp. 12-13, 58, 63 Library of Congress Prints and Photographs Division; pp. 18-19 Kean Collection/Archive Photos/Getty Images; pp. 20, 26-27, 28-29, 37, 47 Library of Congress, Washington, D.C.; p. 23 Interim Archives/ Archive Photos/Getty Images; p. 30 Education Images/Universal Images Group/Getty Images; p. 34 Rare Book and Special Collections Division, Library of Congress, Washington, D.C.; p. 39 SuperStock/ Getty Images; p. 49 Library of Congress, Rare Book Division, Washington, D.C.; pp. 54-55 Yale Center for British Art, Paul Mellon Collection, USA/Bridgeman Images; p. 56 Rare Books and Manuscripts Division, The New York Public Library, Astor Lenox and Tilden Foundations; p. 61 Private Collection/ Peter Newark American Pictures/Bridgeman Images; p. 65 NARA

CONTENTS

INTRODUCTION

When considering the history of the United States, many people begin with an era known as the Colonial Period, even though the land was inhabited long before then. The Colonial Period was a time when Europeans traveled to the New World to establish permanent settlements.

The 13 colonies were a group of settlements that became the original states of the United States of America. Nearly all the colonies were founded by the English, and all were located along the East Coast of North America. In 1776 the 13 colonies declared their independence from Great Britain. The names of the colonies were Connecticut, Delaware, Georgia, Maryland, Massachusetts, New Hampshire, New Jersey, New York, North Carolina, Pennsylvania, Rhode Island, South Carolina, and Virginia.

In 1607 English settlers founded Jamestown, Virginia, the first permanent English settlement in North America, and in 1624 Virginia became a royal colony. The Puritans known as the Pilgrims founded Plymouth, the second English colony in America, in 1620. New Hampshire was settled in 1623, but it did not gain its name until 1629.

In 1630 another group of Puritans founded the Massachusetts Bay Colony. Massachusetts

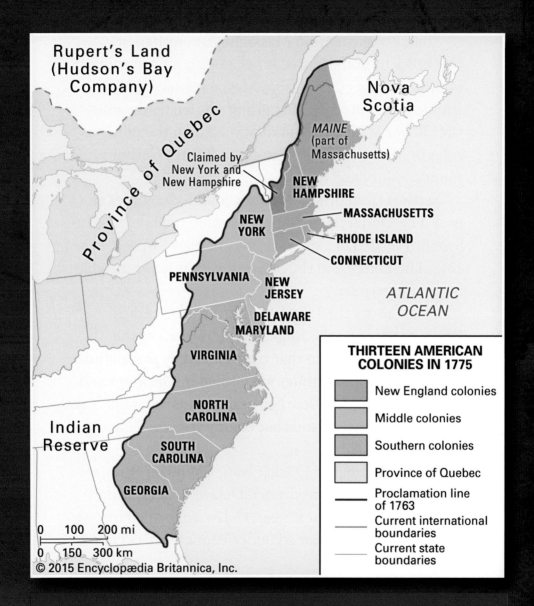

Rupert's Land
(Hudson's Bay
Company)

Nova
Scotia

Province of Quebec

MAINE
(part of
Massachusetts)

Claimed by
New York and
New Hampshire

NEW
HAMPSHIRE

MASSACHUSETTS

NEW
YORK

RHODE ISLAND

CONNECTICUT

PENNSYLVANIA

NEW
JERSEY

ATLANTIC
OCEAN

DELAWARE
MARYLAND

VIRGINIA

Indian
Reserve

NORTH
CAROLINA

SOUTH
CAROLINA

GEORGIA

**THIRTEEN AMERICAN
COLONIES IN 1775**

New England colonies

Middle colonies

Southern colonies

Province of Quebec

Proclamation line
of 1763

Current international
boundaries

Current state
boundaries

0   100   200 mi

0   150   300 km

© 2015 Encyclopædia Britannica, Inc.

The 13 American colonies can be grouped into three regions: New
England, Middle, and Southern. Although they had different governments,
populations, and economies, they eventually banded together.

controlled New Hampshire from 1641 to 1679, and in 1691 Plymouth was joined with Massachusetts.

Some colonists from Massachusetts settled in Connecticut in the 1630s. It became an official colony in 1662. Another group from Massachusetts founded Rhode Island in 1636. That group was led by the minister Roger Williams, who disagreed with the religious rules of Massachusetts. A group of Roman Catholics founded Maryland in 1634.

Settlers from other countries founded colonies as well. The Dutch founded New Netherland in 1624. The Swedish settled in Delaware, part of New Sweden, in 1638. The Dutch and the Swedish also moved into what is now New Jersey.

In the 1650s the Dutch took over the Swedish lands, but in 1664 the English took over all of the Dutch territory. From that time until they gained independence, all the colonies were ruled by the kings and queens of England. New Netherland was renamed New York by the British, and that colony governed New Jersey until 1738.

In 1681 an English Quaker leader, William Penn, set up the colony of Pennsylvania. Delaware became part of Pennsylvania the next year. Delaware formed its own government but remained under Pennsylvania's control until independence.

The Carolina region had become an English colony in 1663. In 1729 Carolina was split into North and South Carolina. Georgia, the last of the original 13 colonies, was settled in 1733.

For most of the time that the colonies were under British rule, the monarchy allowed them a great deal of freedom. Most of the colonies set up forms of self-government. The colonists also developed their own society and economy.

Relations between Britain and the American colonies grew worse after the French and Indian War (1754–63). The British wanted the colonists to pay taxes to help pay for the war, but the colonists did not want to pay taxes without being represented in the British Parliament. These disagreements led to the American Revolution and eventual independence for the 13 colonies.

CHAPTER ONE

FOUNDING OF THE 13 COLONIES

European exploration of the New World began in the late 15th century, with the goal of finding a water passage to Asia. The first expeditions to North America explored the continent's coastlines, and those that followed embarked on expeditions deeper into the interior. Eventually, explorers were sent to the New World to establish colonies.

The first English attempts to establish a colony in the New World failed. In July 1587 a party under John White landed at Roanoke Island off the coast of North Carolina. The following month White sailed back to England. When he returned three years later the entire settlement had disappeared. No one knows what happened to the colonists.

The first permanent English settlement in North America was organized by the London Company (later called the Virginia Company). On May 14, 1607, a group of 105 colonists landed in Virginia and established

Jamestown. Here they built huts for homes, a store-house, a church, and a fort. The strong leadership of Captain John Smith protected the colony from starvation and unfriendly Indians. One of Virginia's chief sources of wealth was the growing of tobacco.

By 1619 Virginia was secure enough to organize the first representative assembly in America. This was the House of Burgesses (or citizens). Its 22 members passed local laws. To further strengthen the colony a shipload of young women arrived in 1619. The settlers then selected wives from among these newcomers.

Located in Virginia, Jamestown was England's first permanent settlement in the New World. It was a fort in the shape of a triangle, with wooden walls protecting a storehouse, a church, and houses. Captain John Smith proved an able leader.

THE NEW ENGLAND COLONIES

The second English colony to be established in America was Plymouth, in 1620. On December 21, more than 100 colonists landed at Plymouth Rock in what is now Massachusetts. The core group among the founders of Plymouth was the Pilgrims. They were Puritans—Protestants who disagreed with some practices of England's official church, the Church of England. Persecuted for their beliefs, they fled England in search of religious freedom. The Pilgrims are also known as Separatists because they chose to "separate" from the Church of England. Their ship was the *Mayflower*. Before they left the ship, the Plymouth settlers adopted the Mayflower Compact, the first plan for self-government in the New World.

In 1620, the first year of settlement, nearly half the settlers died of malnutrition or disease. From that time forward, however, despite

The weary Pilgrims landed on the shores of Plymouth, Massachusetts, on December 21, 1620, after a long and treacherous journey.

decreasing support from English investors, the health and the economic position of the colonists improved. They soon secured peace treaties with most of the Indians around them, enabling them to devote their time to building a strong, stable economic base rather than diverting their efforts toward costly and time-consuming problems of defending the colony from attack. Although none of their main economic activities—farming, fishing, and trading—promised them great wealth, they were, after only five years in America, self-sufficient.

Another group of Puritans founded the Massachusetts Bay Colony in 1630. Like the Pilgrims, they sailed to

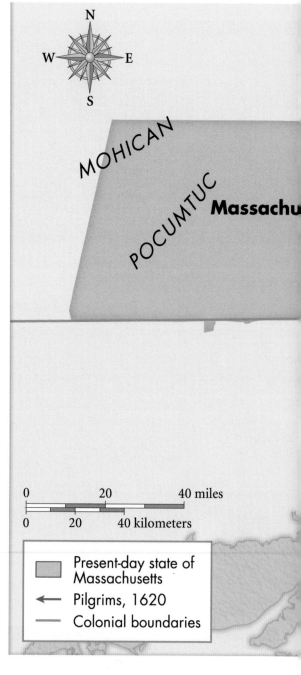

0   20   40 miles

0   20   40 kilometers

Present-day state of Massachusetts

← Pilgrims, 1620

— Colonial boundaries

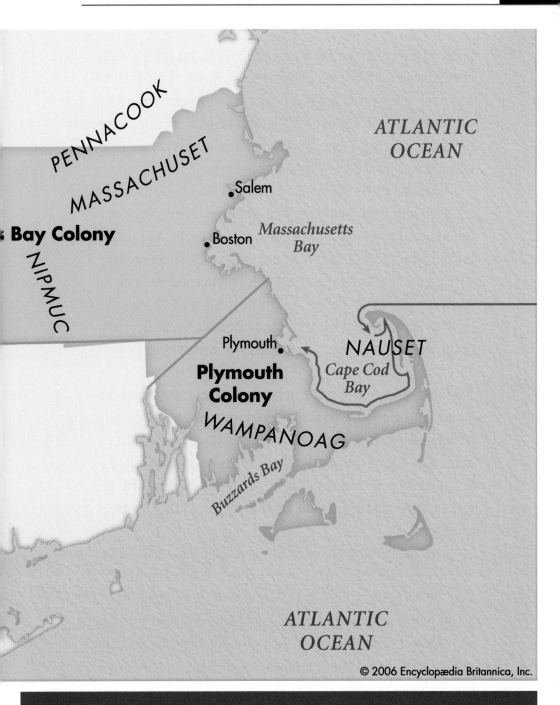

PENNACOOK

MASSACHUSET

Bay Colony

NIPMUC

Salem

Boston

Massachusetts
Bay

ATLANTIC
OCEAN

Plymouth

Plymouth
Colony

WAMPANOAG

NAUSET

Cape Cod
Bay

Buzzards Bay

ATLANTIC
OCEAN

© 2006 Encyclopædia Britannica, Inc.

The Plymouth and Massachusetts Bay colonies are shown on this map of the present-day state of Massachusetts. The red arrow charts the course taken by the Pilgrims on the *Mayflower*.

America mainly to free themselves from religious restraints. Unlike the Pilgrims, however, the Puritans of Massachusetts did not want to separate themselves from the Church of England but, rather, hoped by their example to reform it. In 1691 Plymouth colony was joined to Massachusetts.

The Puritans had a strict moral and religious code that influenced every aspect of their lives. Anyone who failed to live by this code was treated harshly or expelled from the settlement. Some Puritans who disagreed with these policies left Massachusetts to found new settlements. Connecticut was founded by the Reverend Thomas Hooker and his followers after they broke away from Massachusetts in 1635. In the next year Roger Williams, banished from Massachusetts in part for his belief in religious freedom, founded the town of Providence and the colony of Rhode Island. Providence became a haven for Baptists, Quakers, and others who had previously been unable to express their religious beliefs. In 1662 Connecticut and Rhode Island merged under one charter.

The early settlers of New Hampshire and Maine were also ruled by the government of Massachusetts Bay. New Hampshire was permanently separated from Massachusetts in 1692, although it was not until 1741 that it was given its own royal governor. Maine remained under the jurisdiction of Massachusetts until 1820.

THE MIDDLE COLONIES

New Netherland, founded in 1624 at Fort Orange (now Albany, New York) by the Dutch West India Company, was but one element in a wider program of Dutch expansion in the first half of the 17th century. In 1664 the English captured the colony of New Netherland, renaming it New York. In 1685 New York became a royal colony. In 1688 the colony, along with the New England and New Jersey colonies, was made part of the ill-fated Dominion of New England. In 1691 Jacob Leisler, a German merchant living on Long Island, led a successful revolt that resulted in the destruction of the dominion.

Pennsylvania was the most diverse, dynamic, and prosperous of all the North American colonies. Its founder, William Penn, was a Quaker but also a liberal. He gave his colony a democratic form of government and welcomed members of all religious faiths and also those who had no religion.

Penn received his grant of land along the Delaware River in 1681 from King Charles II as a reward for his father's service to the crown. Pennsylvania prospered from the outset. Economic opportunity in Pennsylvania was on the whole greater than in any other colony. Beginning in 1683 with the immigration of Germans into the Delaware River valley and continuing with an enormous influx of Irish and Scotch-Irish in the 1720s and 1730s, the population

Philip Carteret arrives at the colony of New Jersey in 1665 to serve as its first royal governor. Carteret was a cousin of Sir George Carteret, one of the New Jersey colony's proprietors.

of Pennsylvania increased and diversified. The fertile soil of the countryside, in conjunction with a generous government land policy, kept immigration at high levels throughout the 18th century.

New Jersey remained in the shadow of both New York and Pennsylvania throughout most of the colonial period. The area was at one point divided into East Jersey, controlled by George Carteret, and West Jersey, controlled by William Penn and two other Quaker trustees. In 1682 the Quakers bought East Jersey. A multiplicity of owners and an uncertainty of administration caused both colonists and colonizers to feel dissatisfied with the proprietary arrangement, and in 1702 the crown united the two Jerseys into a single royal colony under the governor of New York. It was separated from New York and given its own governor in 1738.

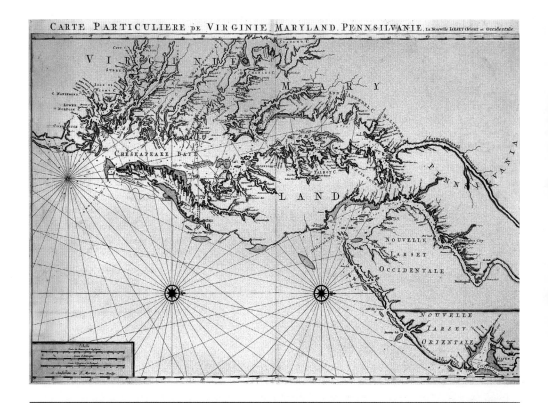

A map dating from about 1700 shows Maryland and surrounding colonies.

When the Quakers purchased East Jersey in 1682, they also acquired the tract of land that was to become Delaware. The purpose of this acquisition was to protect their water route to Pennsylvania. That territory remained part of the Pennsylvania colony until 1704, when it was given an assembly of its own. It remained under the Pennsylvania governor, however, until the American Revolution.

WILLIAM PENN

Born on October 14, 1644, in London, William Penn rebelled against the Church of England early on. He was expelled from university and jailed several times for his Quaker beliefs. Penn wrote pamphlets and books, including *The Sandy Foundation Shaken* (1668) and *No Cross, No Crown (1669)*, advocating Quaker doctrines.

In 1681 King Charles II granted Penn the province of Pennsylvania. It meant a new life for English Quakers. The Quakers were regarded as undesirable both in England and in the already established American colonies. In Pennsylvania they found a home. Penn gave them a popular government, with the right to elect an assembly to make the colony's laws.

Soon after his arrival in Pennsylvania in 1682, Penn started dealings with the Delaware Indians. Several treaties of friendship were made. After two years he was called to England on business. When he returned he found the colony changed. Twenty thousand people now lived in Pennsylvania, and many of them knew nothing of Penn except that he owned their colony and held rights that they wanted. Penn granted their request for an even more democratic government. In 1701 he signed the Charter of Privileges, which remained in force until 1776.

Late in 1701 business again called Penn to England. He never returned to America. His last years were troubled by quarrels with Lord Baltimore, the proprietor of Maryland, by disagreements with many Pennsylvanians, and by the dissolute ways of one of his sons. He died on July 30, 1718, in Buckinghamshire.

THE SOUTHERN COLONIES

Virginia, founded at Jamestown in 1607, was the first of the Southern colonies. The next was Maryland, Virginia's neighbor to the north. It was the first English colony to be controlled by a single proprietor rather than by a joint-stock company. King Charles I granted a charter to George Calvert, the first Lord Baltimore, who wished to found a colony for persecuted Roman Catholics. Calvert died in 1632, however, and the project was taken over by his son Cecilius, the second Lord Baltimore. Cecilius promoted a settlement at St. Mary's on the Potomac River. His younger brother, Leonard, founded the colony in 1634. Supplied in part by Virginia, the Maryland colonists managed to sustain their settlement in modest fashion from the beginning.

The English crown had issued grants to the Carolina territory as early as 1629, but it was not until 1663 that a group of eight proprietors—most of them men of extraordinary wealth and power even by English standards—actually began colonizing the area. The proprietors hoped to grow silk in the warm climate of Carolina, but all efforts to produce that valuable commodity failed. Moreover, it proved difficult to attract settlers to the territory. It was not until 1718, after a series of violent Indian wars had subsided, that the population began to increase substantially. The pattern of settlement, once begun, followed two paths. North Carolina developed into a colony of small to medium farms. South Carolina produced rice and indigo for a world market. The early settlers in both areas came primarily from the West Indian colonies. In 1729 Carolina was split into the two separate royal colonies of North and South Carolina.

The proprietors of Georgia, led by James Oglethorpe, were wealthy English gentlemen. It was Oglethorpe's plan to transport imprisoned debtors to Georgia, where they could rehabilitate themselves by profitable labor and make money for the proprietors in the process. Georgia's economy did not live up to the expectations of the colony's promoters, however.

General James Oglethorpe shakes the hands of local Indians in his new colony of Georgia. A great philanthropist, Oglethorpe hoped to give English debtors a chance for reform by moving them to Georgia.

The silk industry in Georgia, like that in the Carolinas, failed to produce even one profitable crop.

The settlers were also dissatisfied with the lack of self-government in the colony. As protests against the proprietors' policies mounted, the crown in 1752 assumed control over the colony. After that, many of the restrictions that the settlers had complained about, notably those discouraging the institution of slavery, were lifted.

It is important to note that at this point, the 13 colonies were distinct entities, with their own very different governments, cultures, and leaders. The colonists were trying to establish their place in the New World. There was little communication between colonies and certainly no grand idea that they would one day form their own independent nation.

CHAPTER TWO

LIFE IN THE AMERICAN COLONIES

I n the scattered settlements along the Atlantic coast there was steady, if sometimes slow, progress in the daily lives of the colonists. Gains were made in such areas as religious freedom, education, travel, communication, and self-government. The population increased rapidly. Colonial families were generally large, often with 10 to 12 children. At the same time, settlers from Europe continued to find homes in the New World. Most of the early immigrants were English. Then came many from Scotland, Ireland, Germany, and France. In 1690 there were about 250,000 people in the 13 colonies. By 1776, when independence was declared, the population had increased to about 2,500,000.

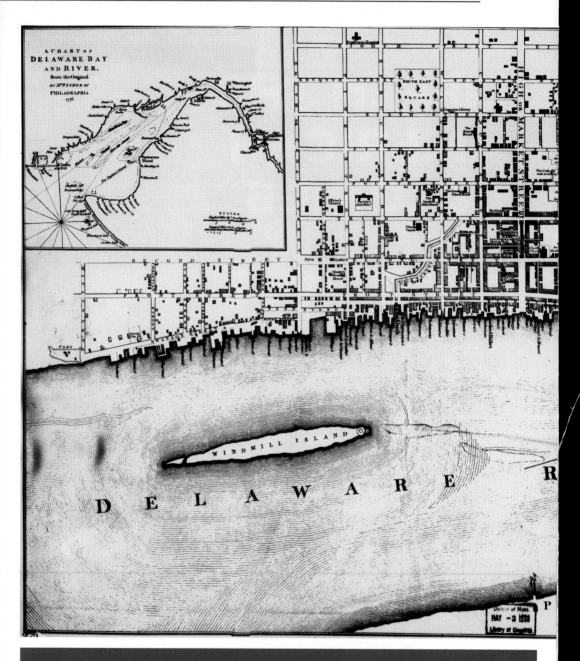

The population of the American colonies grew substantially in the 1700s. This 1776 map depicts Philadelphia, which at the time was the largest city in the colonies with about 30,000 residents.

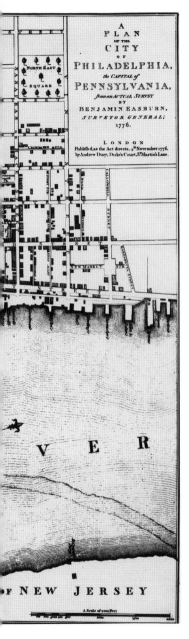

ECONOMY

New England's cold climate and rocky landscape made farming difficult. Although colonial families kept small farms to provide food for themselves, the most successful New Englanders made a living through trade, seafaring, fishing, or craftsmanship. The forests yielded lumber for building ships, which the colonists used for fishing and for trade with Europe, Africa, and the West Indies. New England eventually turned most of its agricultural land over to the raising of livestock. Meat products and fish were valuable exports.

The middle colonies had a milder climate and better farmland than New England. The region produced enough wheat, corn, and other grains to feed the colonies and to export to England. They also built mills to grind the grain into flour. By 1700 Philadelphia exported more than 350,000 bushels of wheat and more than 18,000 tons of flour annually. In addition to fertile farmland, the natural resources of the middle colonies included iron ore and wood from the forests. Factories

b

Tobacco was a major cash crop in the Southern colonies. Harvests were transported by boat to ports for export to England.

produced iron goods, paper, and textiles. Shipbuilding was important as well. Philadelphia and New York flourished as centers of trade.

The founders of the Southern colonies were interested mainly in making profits through large-scale agriculture. They had some key advantages to help them in their goal: a warm climate, fertile soil, and a long growing season. Southerners established huge farms called plantations, which came to dominate the economy. South Carolina produced vast crops of rice and indigo, while Virginia and Maryland specialized in tobacco.

DAILY LIFE

Life in the colonies was challenging, especially in the early years. Coming from established European communities, the settlers did not know how to live in the wilderness. They were not skilled at hunting and fishing, and they suffered from malnutrition and disease. Over time, however, the colonists learned to live off the land, some with the help of Indian tribes. By the 1700s the colonists had established towns and small cities.

Colonial America was mainly a land of farmers. Although each colony had its merchants and craftsmen, most people worked the soil. Some held their own farms, while others worked for a landowner. On the small family farms of New England, all family members did their share of the work. The men planted crops, built fences, and butchered livestock. They also often hunted and fished to feed their families. The women milked the cows, gathered eggs, and preserved food for winter.

As this reenactment from Colonial Williamsburg shows, the colonists worked very hard to sustain their settlements in order to achieve economic success.

They raised the children and did a great number of household chores, including cooking, spinning thread, sewing clothes, making candles and soap, and washing clothes. Boys worked with their fathers, and girls helped their mothers.

In the Southern colonies, with their large plantations, much of the work was done by indentured servants and slaves. Indentured servants agreed to work a number of years for a person who had paid their way to the New World. The typical term of service was from five to seven years, after which the servant became free. Perhaps as many as half of all the white settlers in North America were indentured servants. The first Africans in the Americas, who arrived in Virginia in 1619, were also indentured servants. But plantation owners soon grew dissatisfied with this system of labor. Even as their farms grew and the workload increased, they lost their laborers as the terms of service ended. It was then that they turned to slavery, which provided workers for life. Virginia legalized the practice in 1661

and took the lead in singling out Africans for permanent servitude.

SOCIAL AND POLITICAL STRUCTURE

Over time, England's control over the colonies weak-
ened as the power of colonial leaders grew. One reason
for this shift in power was the distance separating
England and America. Another was the powerful pressures that Americans exerted on royal officials. During
the 1700s the colonial legislatures took responsibility
for legislation affecting taxation and defense and even
took control over the salaries paid to royal officials.
Colonial leaders also gained influence over the appoint-
ment of local officials, which was officially under the
control of the royal governor.

Thus, by the mid-1700s most political power in
America was concentrated in the hands of colonial rather
than royal officials. Although these colonial leaders surely
represented the interests of the colonists better than
any royal official could, the politics of colonial America
were hardly democratic by modern standards. In general,
both social prestige and political power were determined
by wealth, and the wealth of colonial America was controlled by relatively few men.

In the Southern colonies, wealth was concentrated
in the hands of plantation owners. A small group of
planters formed an elite class that dominated local

government. This great concentration of power in the hands of a wealthy few occurred even in Virginia, which pioneered democracy in the colonies by forming the House of Burgesses in 1619. Almost all free adult male Virginians were able to participate in the political process. Nevertheless, the citizens continued to grant power to the elite, whom they considered to be their "betters."

In New England, government was more democratic than in the South. Nearly all free adult male New Englanders could take part in town meetings, which made decisions for the community. Still, a relatively small group of men dominated local affairs. This elite group consisted of men in prominent occupations — notably merchants, lawyers, and clergymen.

The social and political structure of the middle colonies was more diverse than that of any other region in America. In New York, large landowning families exercised a great amount of economic and political power. By contrast, Pennsylvania's government was more open and responsive than that of any other colony in America. The citizens elected representatives to an assembly that made the colony's laws.

CULTURE AND RELIGION

Intellectual life in the colonies focused mainly on applied science. The most famous intellectual of colonial America was Benjamin Franklin. Alongside his talents as a publisher, diplomat, and philosopher, he was a scientist

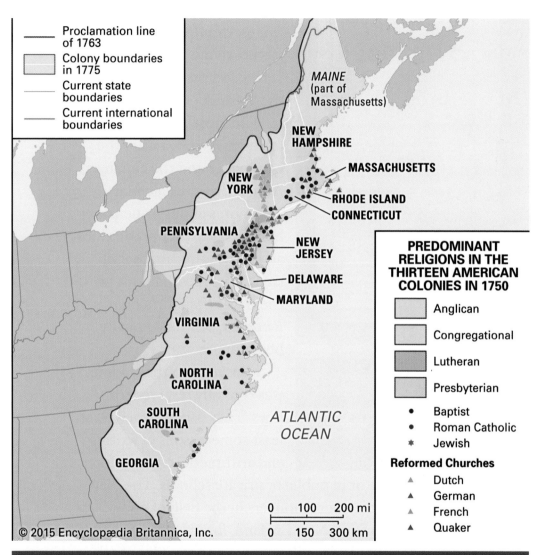

Proclamation line of 1763
Colony boundaries in 1775
Current state boundaries
Current international boundaries

MAINE (part of Massachusetts)

NEW HAMPSHIRE

MASSACHUSETTS

NEW YORK

RHODE ISLAND
CONNECTICUT

PENNSYLVANIA

NEW JERSEY

DELAWARE

MARYLAND

VIRGINIA

NORTH CAROLINA

SOUTH CAROLINA

ATLANTIC OCEAN

GEORGIA

0   100   200 mi
0   150   300 km

© 2015 Encyclopædia Britannica, Inc.

PREDOMINANT RELIGIONS IN THE THIRTEEN AMERICAN COLONIES IN 1750

Anglican
Congregational
Lutheran
Presbyterian
• Baptist
• Roman Catholic
✴ Jewish
Reformed Churches
▲ Dutch
▲ German
▲ French
▲ Quaker

A variety of religions were practiced in the 13 colonies. New England was dominated by Congregationalists, particularly the Puritans. The Middle colonies had great religious diversity. Anglicanism was predominant in the Southern colonies.

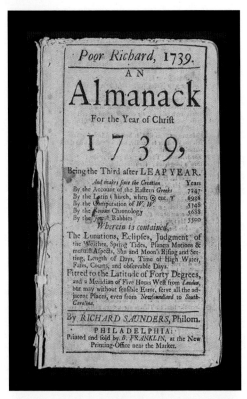

This is the title page for *Poor Richard's* almanac, published for the year 1739. The annual almanac was written, printed, and sold by Benjamin Franklin.

who used his research for practical purposes. His work led, for example, to the manufacture of more efficient stoves and the development of the lightning rod.

The most popular literary forms in America were the newspaper and the almanac. Almanacs were calendars with notes about principal holidays, weather predictions, and astronomical observations. The most famous of them was Franklin's *Poor Richard's*, printed annually beginning in 1732.

Education in the colonies was typically reserved for boys. They usually received at least some lessons in writing and arithmetic, either informally at home or in public or private schools. The New England colonies were pioneers in the field of public education. Outside New England, formal education was generally limited to families who could afford to send their children to private schools. Girls rarely received any formal education. They were taught to perform the duties required to run a household. Colleges and universities served the upper class almost exclusively.

POOR RICHARD

Poor Richard, an unschooled but experienced home-spun philosopher, was a character created by Benjamin Franklin and used as his pen name for the annual *Poor Richard's* almanac, edited by Franklin from 1732 to 1757. Although the Poor Richard of the early almanacs was a dim-witted and foolish astronomer, he was soon replaced by Franklin's famous Poor Richard, a country dweller, dutifully pious, quiet, and rather dull, who is a rich source of prudent and witty sayings on the value of thrift, hard work, and the simple life. Among his practical proverbs are "God helps those who help themselves" and "Early to bed and early to rise, makes a man healthy, wealthy, and wise."

Religion was an important influence on colonial life. This was especially true in New England, with its strong Puritan presence. The middle and Southern colonies were generally more diverse and tolerant in their religious life. Quakers, Lutherans, Presbyterians, Roman Catholics, Baptists, and Anglicans were among the many religious groups found in these regions.

By the early 1700s religious life in the American colonies had lost some of its original zeal as economic prosperity increased and the hardships of the founding era faded in memory. But then came a shake-up—the Great Awakening. This religious revival was a reaction

JONATHAN EDWARDS

One of the biggest names of the Great Awakening was Jonathan Edwards. New England Puritanism never had a more able or eloquent spokesman, nor conservative Christianity in America a more articulate defender. Edwards is still considered one of the most brilliant theological minds ever produced in North America.

Edwards was born in Connecticut in 1703 and graduated from Yale College, where he studied theology. After a short time as a pastor in New York, Edwards served congregations in Massachusetts before moving on to become president of the College of New Jersey (now Princeton University). He had just taken up his duties there when he caught smallpox and died on March 22, 1758.

The Puritanism of Edwards' day had become an easygoing affair that stressed moral self-sufficiency, the good life, and free will while tending to ignore the darker aspects of human nature. It was against this that Edwards directed his attacks and emphasized the goodness of God and faith in Him as the only means of salvation. In his most famous work, *Freedom of Will*, published in 1754, he said that people are free to do as they please and are therefore held morally responsible for their actions. His book *The Nature of True Virtue* (1765) was an important treatise on ethics. His sermons and writings were a major element in the last years of the Great Awakening, the religious revival that lasted from about 1720 into the 1740s. These paved the way for the more far-reaching revival of the early 1800s.

An engraving from about 1740 depicts the College of William and Mary in Williamsburg, Virginia. Chartered in 1693, it was the second college founded in the American colonies. The first was Harvard, founded in Massachusetts in 1636.

against the increasing secularization of colonial society and against the corporate and materialistic nature of the main American churches. In fiery sermons, revivalist preachers emphasized the need for sinners to fear punishment from an all-powerful and angry God. By rejecting worldliness and returning to faith, however, one could hope for a return to God's grace. Among the most popular preachers of the Great Awakening were George Whitefield, Gilbert Tennent, and Jonathan Edwards.

CHAPTER THREE

PRESSURES FROM ABROAD AND AT HOME

The American colonies, though in many ways isolated from the countries of Europe, were nevertheless continually subject to diplomatic and military pressures from abroad. In particular, Spain and France were always nearby, waiting to exploit any signs of British weakness in America in order to increase their commercial and territorial designs on the North American mainland. Between 1689 and 1748 the two powers waged three separate wars, both in Europe and in America. The first strong attempt to unite the colonies was a farseeing plan adopted by the so-called Albany Congress as a response to a French threat in 1754. The plan was rejected by both the colonies and Great Britain.

The other major players in this struggle for control of North America were the American Indians. When

For a while, the English colonists enjoyed favorable relations with the American Indians already living on the land. Settling colonists knew it was in their best interest to make peace with the Indians and to learn all they could from them.

the English set up their colonies, relations with the Indians were generally peaceful. The Indians allowed the colonists to build, farm, and hunt in certain areas and helped them adjust to their new environment. Both the Indians and the colonists benefited from trade with one another. Within a few years, however, the colonists' desire for land and their disregard for the Indians caused relations to deteriorate. In time, conflict was inevitable.

THE FRENCH AND INDIAN WAR

Between 1689 and 1748 England and France waged three separate wars—King William's War, Queen Anne's War, and King George's War—over their interests in North America. The two powers vied for control over the Indians, for possession of the territory lying to the north of the North American colonies, for access to the trade in the Northwest, and for commercial superiority in the West Indies. In most of these encounters, France had been aided by Spain. Because of its own holdings immediately south and west of the British colonies and in the Caribbean, Spain realized that it was in its own interest to join with the French in limiting British expansion. In addition, both the French and the British were helped in these conflicts by their American Indian allies.

The culmination of these struggles came in 1754 with the French and Indian War. Whereas previous contests between Great Britain and France in North America had been mostly provincial affairs, with American colonists doing most of the fighting for the British, the French and Indian War saw sizable commitments of British troops to America. The strategy of the British under William Pitt was to allow their ally, Prussia, to carry the brunt of the fighting in Europe and thus free Britain to concentrate its troops in America.

Despite the fact that they were outnumbered 15 to 1 by the British colonial population in America, the French were nevertheless well equipped to hold their own. They had a larger military organization in America than did the English, their troops were better trained, and they were more successful than the British in forming military alliances with the Indians. The early engagements of the war went to the French. The surrender of George Washington to a superior French force at Fort Necessity, the annihilation of General Edward Braddock at the Monongahela River,

In 1755, the French and their Native American allies ambushed Edward Braddock's British and colonial troops along the Monongahela River. The British troops had been on their way to attack the French-held Fort Duquesne.

and French victories at Oswego and Fort William Henry all made it seem as if the war would be a short and unsuccessful one for the British.

Even as these defeats took place, however, the British were able to increase their supplies of both men and equipment in America. By 1758, with its strength finally up to a satisfactory level, Britain began to implement its larger strategy. It involved sending a combined land and sea force to gain control of the St. Lawrence River and a large land force aimed at Fort Ticonderoga to eliminate French control of Lake Champlain.

The first expedition against the French at Ticonderoga was a disaster, as General James Abercrombie led about 15,000 British and colonial troops in an attack against the French before his forces were adequately prepared. The British assault on Louisburg, the key to the St. Lawrence, was more successful. In July 1758 Lord Jeffrey Amherst led a naval attack in which his troops landed on the shores from small boats, established beachheads, and then captured the fort at Louisburg.

In 1759, after several months of sporadic fighting, the forces of James Wolfe captured Quebec from the French army led by the marquis de Montcalm. This was probably the turning point of the war. By the fall of 1760, the British had taken Montreal, and Britain possessed practical control of all of the North American continent. It took another two years for Britain to defeat its rivals in other parts of the world,

JAMES WOLFE

A British hero of the French and Indian War, James Wolfe was born on January, 2, 1727, in Kent, England. At 14 he entered the army. He rose rapidly by remarkable demonstrations of tactical skill and personal bravery. At 17 he was a captain; at 18, a brigade major; at 22, a lieutenant colonel. Wolfe fought in the War of the Austrian Succession. When it ended in 1748 he was stationed for several years in England and Scotland. Wolfe then took up the studies he had missed in his teens. He learned languages and mathematics and read widely in history and philosophy.

When Prime Minister William Pitt, the Elder, took office he strengthened England's military forces by promoting officers on merit alone. In 1758 he made young Wolfe a brigadier general. Wolfe was sent to America to assist Lord Jeffrey Amherst in the attack on Louisburg. Wolfe's brigade landed under heavy fire, laid siege, and finally took the fort.

A few months later Pitt gave Wolfe command of the Quebec expedition, with the rank of major general. In June 1759 Wolfe arrived in Quebec with a fleet of 140 ships and 9,000 soldiers. Opposing him were the French commanders Louis-Joseph Montcalm and François-Gaston Lévis. They had 6,000 men holding the Beauport shore and a smaller force above the city.

For 12 weeks Wolfe made probing attacks but could gain no ground. Finally on the night of September 12 his troops made a landing 2 miles (3.2 kilometers) above the city. By the next morning the British were ready for battle on the Plains of Abraham. Montcalm brought up his men from Beauport. The seasoned British soldiers under Wolfe broke the French defense in a few hours. Wolfe lived only long enough to learn of the victory. He died on September 13. Montcalm likewise was mortally wounded.

French soldier Louis-Joseph Montcalm was defeated on the Plains of Abraham by an army commanded by British General James Wolfe. Both Montcalm and Wolfe were mortally wounded at the battle.

but the contest for control of North America had been settled.

In the Treaty of Paris of 1763, Great Britain took possession of all of Canada, East and West Florida, all territory east of the Mississippi in North America, and St. Vincent, Tobago, and Dominica in the Caribbean. At the time, the British victory seemed one of the greatest in its history. The British Empire in North America had been not only secured but also greatly expanded. It was now certain that English speech and customs would prevail in the future United States.

Almost immediately, however, conflicts arose as the needs and interests of the British Empire began to differ from those of the American colonies. The colonies, now economically powerful, culturally distinct, and steadily becoming more independent politically, would ultimately rebel before submitting to the British plan of empire. The first strong attempt to unite the colonies

ALBANY CONGRESS

From June 19 to July 11, 1754, an intercolonial conference was held at Albany, New York. Present were 23 delegates from the English colonies of New York, Pennsylvania, New Hampshire, Connecticut, Massachusetts, Rhode Island, and Maryland, along with 150 members of the Iroquois Indian federation. The Albany Congress had been called by the English Board of Trade to deal with two pressing issues: grievances of the Iroquois against the colonies and the presence of hostile French forces and their Indian allies to the west of the English colonies.

The Indians complained to the congress that land speculators were stealing their lands; that an illegal English-French trade was bypassing them, thus preventing them from acting as middlemen for profit; and that colonists were trading directly with other Indians supposedly under the rule of the Iroquois. The congress had to placate the Iroquois, because they were needed as allies against the French.

More serious was the French threat. To meet it, the congress drew up a plan of colonial union. Written mainly by Benjamin Franklin, the plan provided for one general government for all the colonies to manage defense and Indian affairs, pass laws, and raise taxes. The chief executive was to be a president general appointed by the king of England. The legislature, or grand council, would consist of representatives appointed by the colonial legislatures.

The Albany plan of colonial union failed because of opposition from both the king and the colonies: each thought it granted the other too much power. It was, nevertheless, a farsighted document. It contained solutions that the colonies would draw upon in forming a union after independence was declared in 1776.

had already been made in response to the French threat. In 1754 colonial representatives gathered at the Albany Congress, which adopted a plan of colonial union for security and defense against the French. The plan was largely the work of Benjamin Franklin. Although it was rejected by both the colonies and Great Britain, it looked forward to the colonies' eventual unification.

This 1754 political cartoon by Benjamin Franklin was a warning to the British colonies in America to unite against the French and Indians. The segmented snake represents the colonies, "S.C., N.C., V., M., R., N.J., N.Y., [and] N.E."

COLONIALISM AND THE NATIVE AMERICANS

In dealing with the Native Americans, the English colonizers significantly differed from the Spanish and French. Spain's widespread empire in the Southwest relied on scattered garrisons and missions to keep the Indians under control and "usefully" occupied. The French in Canada dealt with the Indians essentially as the source of fur. The English colonies encouraged the immigration of an agricultural population that required large land areas to cultivate—which had to be secured from the Indians.

English colonial officials began by making land purchases, but such transactions worked to the disadvantage of the Indians. To the Indians, who had no concept of private landownership, the very idea of a land "sale" was foreign. While the English believed they were purchasing the land outright, the Indians thought they were agreeing only to share or rent the land. After a "sale" was concluded, they were surprised to learn that they had given up their hunting and fishing rights.

In the early days of settlement, cooperation between the Indians and the Europeans could and did take place. Two well-known examples were the assistance given by Squanto to the settlers of Plymouth colony and the marriage of Virginia's John Rolfe to Pocahontas, the daughter of Chief Powhatan. The Native Americans taught the newcomers techniques of survival in their new environment and in turn were introduced to and quickly adopted metal utensils, European fabrics, and especially firearms. In land transactions, however, the Europeans used two key advantages—a common written language and a modern system of exchange—to turn purchases into thinly disguised land grabs. William Penn and Roger Williams made particular efforts to deal fairly with the Native Americans, but they were rare exceptions.

The impact of Indian involvement in the affairs of the colonists was especially evident in the struggle between France and Britain over Canada. For furs the

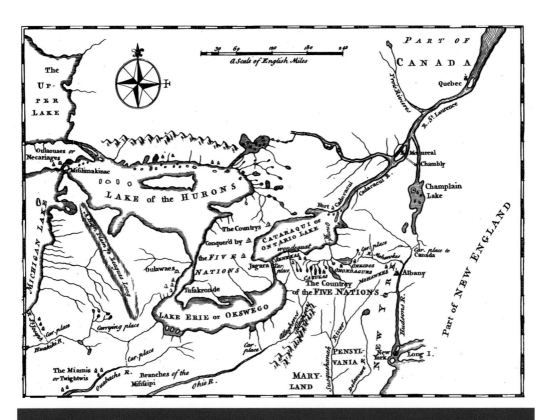

A map from the 1700s shows the location of the original five nations of the Iroquois Confederacy.

French had depended on the Huron people settled around the Great Lakes, but the Iroquois Confederacy, based in western New York and southern Ontario, succeeded in crushing the Huron and drove Huron allies such as the Susquehannock and the Delaware southward into Pennsylvania. This action put the British in debt to the Iroquois because it diverted some of the fur trade from French Montreal and Quebec City to British Albany and New York City. European-Indian alliances also affected the way in which the Choctaw, influenced by the French in Louisiana, battled with

The Ottawa chief Pontiac meets with Major Robert Rogers, commander of a British-American militia force, in the 1700s. In 1763 Pontiac led a coalition of tribes in a rebellion against British power in the Great Lakes region.

Spanish-supported Apalachee from Florida and with the Cherokee, who were armed by the British in Georgia.

The French and Indian War produced several Indian leaders, such as Red Jacket and Joseph Brant, who were competent in two or three languages and could negotiate deals between their own peoples and the Europeans. But the climactic struggle between France and Britain was the beginning of disaster for the Indians. When the English succeeded in driving the French from Canada, the Indians could no longer use the strategy of supporting whichever king—English or French—would restrain westward settlement. This realization led some Indians to consider mounting a united resistance to further colonial expansion. In 1763 the Ottawa chief Pontiac led such a rebellion. However, like later Indian challenges to European and then U.S. power, it was simply not enough.

CHAPTER FOUR

PRELUDE TO REVOLUTION

B ritain's victory over France in the French and Indian War came at a great cost. British government spending more than doubled during the war. It therefore seemed reasonable to the British that some of the future costs of defending the colonies should be shifted to the colonists themselves—who until then had been lightly taxed. The war also made Britain realize it needed to be involved more closely in governing the colonies.

THE PROCLAMATION OF 1763

At the end of the French and Indian War, the British crown declared the Proclamation of 1763. The proclamation drew a line down the Appalachian Mountains, from south of Hudson Bay to north of the Floridas, marking the limit of settlement from the British colonies. The proclamation thus made the land west of the Appalachians into a vast British-administered Indian reservation. It forbade colonial settlement on that land, ordered those settlers already there to withdraw, and strictly limited future settlement. In the Indian territory, trade with the Indians was to be conducted strictly through British-appointed commissioners.

The proclamation was mainly intended to placate the Indians, but it also greatly angered the colonists. They objected to what they considered the British government's interference in their affairs and resented the limits on settlement and speculation in the western lands. The most ambitious men in the colonies saw the proclamation as a loss of power to control their own fortunes. Colonial resentment over the halt in westward expansion was one of the factors in sparking the crisis that led to revolution.

TAX CONTROVERSIES

To meet the costs of colonial defense, the British Parliament began instituting a series of tax measures to collect money from the colonies. The first, in 1764, was the Sugar Act. It was aimed at ending the smuggling trade in sugar and molasses from the French and Dutch West Indies. The Sugar Act provided for strong customs enforcement of the duties

Colonists used sugar and molasses smuggled in from the French and Dutch West Indies. With the enforcement of the Sugar Act, shipments of sugar and molasses from non-British sources were subject to a high tax and possible seizure.

on refined sugar and molasses imported into the colonies from non-British Caribbean sources. The colonies reacted by protesting. It was not just the tax that they objected to. They also resented that shipmasters could be punished and their cargoes seized if they violated the trade rules.

Since the new Sugar Act would not afford a large revenue, it was supplemented in 1765 by the Stamp Act. This measure levied a direct tax on all newspapers printed in the colonies and on most commercial and legal documents used in business. It was realized that these two revenue acts would provide less than half the money needed for the army. Another measure—the Quartering Act—required each colony to bear part of the expenses incurred by British troops when stationed or moving within its borders. The Currency Act of 1764 increased the load of taxes to be carried by the colonists. This act directed the colonists to pay, within a fairly short time, the whole domestic debt that they had created in waging the French and Indian War.

Opposition to the Stamp Act spread through the colonial assemblies, especially that of Virginia. People in Boston and later other colonies formed groups known as the Sons of Liberty to protest the act. The opposition came to a head in the Stamp Act Congress of 1765, which asserted that the colonists, as English subjects, could not be taxed without their consent. Alarmed by the refusal of the colonial towns to buy additional goods while the act remained in force, British merchants petitioned Parliament for its repeal. The Stamp Act was repealed in 1766. At the same time, however, Parliament declared that it had full power to tax the colonies whenever and however it thought best.

A year later Parliament struck again. From June 15

Newspaper editors believed the Stamp Act would destroy their business, as depicted in this 1765 illustration.

to July 2, 1767, it issued a series of resolutions called the Townshend Acts in yet another attempt to assert its authority and generate revenue in the colonies. The Townshend duties were direct taxes on imported British goods in the colonies such as glass, paper, paint, and tea. With no representation in Parliament, colonial legislative assemblies were limited in their abilities to contest the Townshend Acts. Resistance to the acts followed as colonists withheld payments and staged public demonstrations denouncing the unpopular taxes.

THE BOSTON MASSACRE

In 1770, in the face of heated protests, Parliament repealed all the Townshend Acts except the tax on tea. Although relative calm returned to the colonies, skirmishes between colonists and British soldiers continued along the New England coastline.

One of the most violent clashes occurred in Massachusetts in 1770. On March 5, a crowd of citizens confronted eight British soldiers in the streets of Boston. As the outraged mob insulted and threatened them, the soldiers fired their muskets into the crowd. Five colonists were killed, including a former slave named Crispus Attucks, while several others were wounded. Attucks was the first victim to fall and gained notoriety as one of the first people to die for the cause of independence.

This depiction of the skirmish that came to be known as the Boston Massacre was created by Henry Pelham and engraved by Paul Revere. The portrayal was intentionally sensational in an effort to rile up the already outraged colonists.

The incident soon became known as the Boston Massacre. It would lead to additional acts of retaliation in the colonies against the harsh mandates and heavy taxes imposed by Parliament.

CRISPUS ATTUCKS

The first American to die at the Boston Massacre, Crispus Attucks became a powerful symbol as a martyr in the American colonists' struggle against the British. Attucks's life prior to the day of his death is still shrouded in mystery. Nothing is known for certain, but historians generally agree that Attucks was of mixed ancestry, of both African and Natick Indian descent. It is also believed that Attucks was the runaway slave described in a notice that ran in the *Boston Gazette* in 1750. In the 20-year interval between his escape from slavery and his death at the hands of British soldiers, Attucks probably spent a good deal of time aboard whaling ships.

Attucks was the first to fall at the massacre, his chest pierced by two bullets. His body was carried to Faneuil Hall, where it lay in state until March 8. On the day of the funeral of Attucks and three others, shops closed, and thousands of residents followed the procession to the Granary burial ground, where the men were buried in a common grave. The event was a galvanizing one for the colonists chafing under

(CONTINUED ON THE FOLLOWING PAGE)

(CONTINUED FROM THE PREVIOUS PAGE)

British rule. Pamphleteers and propagandists quickly dubbed it a "massacre."

During the trial of the British soldiers John Adams, who went on to become the second U.S. president, was the defense lawyer. Adams painted Attucks as a troublemaker who was to blame for the soldiers' attack. Testimony varied, with some witnesses saying that Attucks had grabbed at the bayonet of one of the soldiers and was shot in the ensuing struggle; however, others said Attucks was leaning on a stick when shot. The British captain and six of the group were acquitted, including the soldier who had been charged with killing Attucks; two more were found guilty and branded on the thumb.

Attucks was the only victim of the Boston Massacre whose name was widely remembered. For years the people of Boston marked each March 5 as Crispus Attucks Day to commemorate the turning point in the struggle against the British. In 1888 the Crispus Attucks monument was unveiled in Boston.

THE BOSTON TEA PARTY

To evade the remaining Townshend tax on tea, Boston merchants bought tea smuggled into the colonies by Dutch traders. In 1773 Parliament passed the Tea Act, which granted the East India Company the

On December 16, 1773, Boston citizens dressed as Mohawk Indians boarded East India Company ships and destroyed hundreds of chests of tea. This act of rebellion, known as the Boston Tea Party, shocked the British Parliament.

exclusive right to export tea to the colonies. The act also exempted the East India Company from paying an export tax. The company carried the tea in its own ships and sold the tea through its own agents, which enabled it to sell the tea at a lower price than its competitors.

Colonial merchants in cities such as New York and Philadelphia resisted the East India Company's monopoly on tea exports by canceling orders and refusing consignments. In Boston, however, the royal governor, Thomas Hutchinson, was determined to uphold the law. He allowed three East India Company ships to unload their cargoes of tea and required that the merchants in Boston pay the appropriate taxes for the shipments. On the night of December 16, 1773, a group of nearly 60 colonists disguised as Mohawk Indians boarded these ships and tossed 342 chests of tea into Boston Harbor to protest the taxes and the monopoly.

The Boston Tea Party marked the first act of open resistance to British rule. In response, Britain was determined to punish the colonies, particularly Massachusetts.

THE INTOLERABLE ACTS

In the spring of 1774 Parliament passed a series of punitive measures known in the colonies as the Intolerable Acts. These acts closed the port of Boston and canceled the colonial charter of Massachusetts. Massachusetts was reduced to a crown colony and a British military government was instated. The Intolerable Acts also allowed British officials accused of crimes in America to stand trial in Britain and forced colonists to provide additional housing for British troops.

To make matters worse, Parliament also passed the Quebec Act of 1774. This act extended the southern boundary of the Canadian province of Quebec to the Ohio River. The colonists perceived the expansion of Quebec, with its strong French influence, as a threat to colonial stability and unity.

The passage of the Intolerable Acts was another attempt to reimpose strict British control over the

In June 1775 the Second Continental Congress appointed George Washington commander in chief of the Continental Army in the American Revolution.

colonies. But rather than separating Massachusetts from the other colonies as Britain had hoped, the oppressive mandates provoked colonial action to oppose British rule. Representatives from the 13 colonies met to contest the acts in Philadelphia on September 5, 1774, in what became the First Continental Congress.

B y the time the Second Continental Congress opened in 1775, war had begun between the colonies and Britain in Massachusetts. The Congress took over the new American army and put George Washington in charge. It also directed the war effort and acted as the provisional government for the colonies by issuing and borrowing money, setting up a postal service, and creating a navy.

By mid-1776 the conflict was so far along that the Congress gave up on a peaceful settlement. On July 2, the Congress voted to declare the 13 American colonies to be "free and independent states," with no ties to Britain. Then they considered how to announce that fact to the world. By the end of the day on July 4, the final wording

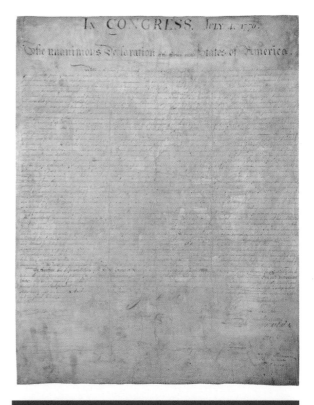

Members of the Second Continental Congress drafted the Declaration of Independence, which announced the separation of the American colonies from Great Britain.

had been determined and the Congress voted to adopt one of history's greatest documents — the Declaration of Independence.

Several years of armed combat secured international recognition of what the declaration had proclaimed: The American colonies became independent of Great Britain and formed the United States of America. The Declaration of Independence has since become a source of pride for the American people, who have embraced it as an enduring symbol of the nation's founding principles.

1587 An English colony is established at Roanoke
    Island. It disappears within three years.

1607 Jamestown, Virginia, the first permanent
    English settlement in North America, is
    founded.

1620 Puritans known as the Pilgrims establish
    Plymouth, America's second English colony.

1623 New Hampshire is settled.

1624 Virginia becomes a royal colony. The Dutch
    establish New Netherland.

1630 The Massachusetts Bay Colony is founded.

1634 Maryland is founded as a haven for Roman
    Catholics.

1635 Colonists from Massachusetts settle in
    Connecticut.

1636 Roger Williams founds Rhode Island.

1638 Swedish settlers establish New Sweden in
    Delaware.

1662 Connecticut becomes an official colony.

1663 Carolina becomes an English colony.

1664 English rule is established over all the
    American colonies.

1681 William Penn establishes the colony of
    Pennsylvania.

1691 The Plymouth and Massachusetts Bay colonies
    are joined.

1729 Carolina colony is split into North Carolina and South Carolina.

1733 Georgia is settled.

1754 The Albany Congress is held from June 19 through July 11. The French and Indian War begins.

1763 The Treaty of Paris, ending the French and Indian War, gives Britain possession of all of Canada, East and West Florida, all territory east of the Mississippi River, and St. Vincent, Tobago, and Dominica in the Caribbean. The Proclamation of 1763 organizes British territories in America and forbids colonial settlement on Indian territory.

1764 Parliament passes the Sugar Act.

1765 Parliament passes the Stamp Act.

1770 The Boston Massacre occurs on March 5.

1773 Parliament passes the Tea Act. The Boston Tea Party takes place on December 16.

1774 First Continental Congress meets.

1775 Second Continental Congress opens.

1776 The Continental Congress adopts the Declaration of Independence on July 4, and the 13 colonies become the United States of America.

GLOSSARY

almanac Annual calendar of important dates and data.

colony An area that is controlled by or belongs to a country and is usually far away from it.

doctrine Principles in a system of belief.

dominion The territory of a government.

expedition A journey undertaken by a group with the purpose of exploration, research, or settlement.

Great Awakening A religious revival that took place in the American colonies from the 1720s to the 1740s. It was a reaction against the reliance on reason as the basis for establishing religious truth and the increasing secularization of society.

materialistic To be concerned with money or material possessions.

Mayflower Compact The first governing document of Plymouth colony.

Pilgrims Also called Separatists, a group of Puritans who fled England and founded the first permanent settlement in New England at Plymouth in 1620.

placate To calm the anger or bitterness of.

proprietor Person to whom ownership of a colony is granted.

punitive Intended to inflict punishment.

Puritans English Protestants of the 1500s and 1600s who opposed many customs of the Church of England.

Quakers A Christian group that stresses the guidance of the Holy Spirit, rejects sacraments and an ordained ministry, and opposes war; also known as the Society of Friends.

religious revival Renewed religious fervor within a Christian group, church, or community.

secularization Transfer of the ownership or control of something from a religious organization to the state.

settlement A place or region to which people have moved and made their home.

Boston Tea Party Ships and Museum
Congress Street Bridge
Boston, MA 02127
(866) 955-0667
Website: http://www.bostonteapartyship.com
This floating museum offers an immersive experi-
    ence of the Boston Tea Party. Visitors are invited to
    join actors portraying the colonists in dumping tea
    overboard.

Bushy Run Battlefield
1253 Bushy Run Road
Jeannette, PA 15644
(724) 527-5584
Website: http://bushyrunbattlefield.com
This battlefield was active during Pontiac's War in
    1763. Battlefield tours and educational programs are
    offered.

Carpenters' Hall
320 Chestnut Street
Philadelphia, PA 19106
(215) 925-0167
Website: http://www.carpentershall.org
Carpenters' Hall hosted the First Continental Congress
    in 1774. The building is open to the public for tours.

Colonial Williamsburg
The Colonial Williamsburg Foundation
P.O. Box 1776
Williamsburg, VA 23187
(888) 965-7254
Website: http://www.colonialwilliamsburg.com
Colonial Williamsburg is a living history museum that
    replicates a colonial-era village. Visitors can interact
    with tradespeople, shopkeepers, and political figures
    to get an idea of what it was like to be a colonist.

Fort Beauséjour – Fort Cumberland National Historic
    Site
111 Fort Beauséjour Road
Aulac, NB E4L 2W5
Canada
(506) 364-5080
Website: http://www.pc.gc.ca/eng/lhn-nhs/nb/beause-
jour/index.aspx
This historic fort was built by the French in 1751. It was
    active during both the conflict between France and
    Britain for control of North America and the later
    American Revolution.

Fort Pitt Museum
Point State Park
601 Commonwealth Place
Pittsburgh, PA 15222
(412) 281-9284

Website: http://www.heinzhistorycenter.org/fort-pitt
This museum, within Point State Park, is a recrea-
    tion of a fort built by the British in 1759, during the
    French and Indian War. Nearby is an outline of Fort
    Duquesne, a French fort of the era.

Fort Ticonderoga
100 Fort Ti Road
Ticonderoga, NY 12883
(518) 585-2821
Website: http://www.fortticonderoga.org
Visitors to Fort Ticonderoga can watch tradesmen at
    work and view a reenactment of the marquis de
    Montcalm's great victory over the British in 1758.

George Washington's Mount Vernon
3200 Mount Vernon Memorial Highway
Mount Vernon, VA 22121
(703) 780-2000
Website: http://www.mountvernon.org
Situated on the banks of the Potomac River, the plan-
    tation estate of George and Martha Washington is
    open to visitors. Guests can tour Washington's man-
    sion and grounds, including his tomb.

Independence National Historical Park
143 South Third Street
Philadelphia, PA 19106
(215) 965-2305

Website: http://www.nps.gov/inde/index.htm
The centerpiece of this park is Independence Hall,
    the building where both the Declaration of
    Independence and the U.S. Constitution were
    signed. The park also houses the Liberty Bell.

The National Museum of American History
14th Street and Constitution Avenue NW
Washington, DC 20001
(202) 633-1000
Website: http://americanhistory.si.edu
The National Museum of American History preserves
    more than 3 million artifacts from colonial times to
    the present. The museum features permanent, tem-
    porary, and online exhibits.

Plimoth Plantation
137 Warren Avenue
Plymouth, MA 02360
(508) 746-1622
Website: http://www.plimoth.org
Plimoth Plantation is a living history museum where
    visitors can experience a reconstruction of the
    Plymouth colony and a Wampanoag Indian home
    site. Plimoth Plantation also features the *Mayflower
    II*, a replica of the ship that brought the Pilgrims to
    America.

Roanoke Island Festival Park
One Festival Park

Manteo, NC 27954
(252) 475-1500
Website: http://www.roanokeisland.com
This interactive history site represents the country's
    first English settlement attempt in North America.
    Visitors can board and explore a reproduction of the
    Elizabeth II, explore a representation of an American
    Indian town, and learn about daily colonial life from
    costumed interpreters.

WEBSITES

Because of the changing nature of Internet links, Rosen
Publishing has developed an online list of websites
related to the subject of this book. This site is updated
regularly. Please use this link to access this list:

http://www.rosenlinks.com/EAH/Col

BIBLIOGRAPHY

Burgan, Michael. *African Americans in the Thirteen Colonies*. New York, NY: Children's Press, 2013.

Caravantes, Peggy. *The French and Indian War.* Minneapolis, MN: ABDO Publishing Company, 2013.

Havelin, Kate. *Buckskin Dresses and Pumpkin Breeches: Colonial Fashions from the 1580s to the 1760s.* Minneapolis, MN: Twenty-First Century Books, 2011.

Hollar, Sherman, ed. *Biographies of Colonial America.* New York, NY: Britannica Educational Publishing, 2013.

Keller, Susanna, ed. *The Age of Exploration.* New York, NY: Britannica Educational Publishing in association with Rosen Educational Services, 2016.

Lacayo, Richard. *Benjamin Franklin.* New York, NY: Time-Life Books, 2010.

Lowery, Zoe, ed. *The American Revolution.* New York, NY: Britannica Educational Publishing in association with Rosen Educational Services, 2016.

Mattern, Joanne. *William Penn.* New York, NY: Chelsea House, 2011.

McNeese, Tim, and Richard Jensen. *Colonial America, 1543–1763.* New York, NY: Chelsea House, 2010.

Nardo, Don. *Daily Life in Colonial America.* Detroit, MI: Lucent Books, 2010.

Nardo, Don. *Government and Social Class in Colonial America*. Detroit, MI: Lucent Books, 2010.

Pederson, Charles E. *The French and Indian War*. Edina, MN: ABDO, 2010.

Pratt, Mary K. *A Timeline History of the Thirteen Colonies*. Minneapolis, MN: Lerner Publications, 2014.

Robson, David. *Colonial America*. San Diego, CA: ReferencePoint Press, 2013.

Slavicek, Louise Chipley. *Anne Hutchinson*. New York, NY: Chelsea House, 2011.

Woolf, Alex. *Finding an Identity: Early America and the Colonial Period, 1492–1774*. New York, NY: Chelsea House, 2011.

INDEX